I work in a Restaurant

by Clare Oliver

Photography by Chris Fairclough

W

FRANKLIN WATTS
LONDON • SYDNEY

© 2001 Franklin Watts

First published in 2001 by
Franklin Watts
96 Leonard Street
London
EC2A 4XD

Franklin Watts Australia
56 O'Riordan Street
Alexandria
NSW 2015

ISBN: 0 7496 4056 1
Dewey Decimal Classification 647.95
A CIP catalogue reference for this book is available
from the British Library

Printed in Malaysia

Editor: Kate Banham
Designer: Joelle Wheelwright
Art Direction: Jason Anscomb
Photography: Chris Fairclough
Consultant: Beverley Mathias, REACH
REACH is the National Advice Centre for Children with Reading
Difficulties. REACH can be contacted at California Country Park,
Nine Mile Ride, Finchampstead, Berkshire RG40 4HT (0118 973 7575).
Check out the website at **www.reach-reading.demon.co.uk** or
email them on **reach@reach-reading.demon.co.uk**.

Acknowledgements
The publishers would like to thank Jacki Griffith and
the staff and customers of Pizza Hut, Briggate, Leeds,
for their help in the production of this book.

Contents

(Note: words printed in **bold italics** are explained in the glossary.)

Meet Jacki

How would you like as many free pizzas as you could eat...every day? That's one of the **perks** of Jacki's job. Jacki is 17 years old and has worked in her local pizza restaurant for nearly three years. It's her first job.

Jacki serves up pizza with a smile.

When she started there, she was still at school, so she worked as a Saturday girl. Now she works full-time. Her boss is Jo, the restaurant's General Manager. When Jo is not there, Jacki reports to Steve, the Assistant Manager.

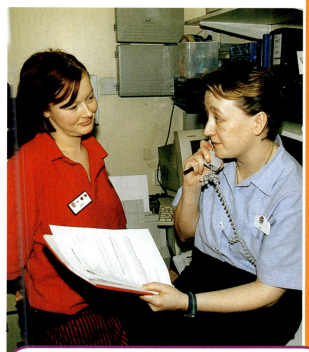

Jo is usually in the restaurant office. Jacki goes to see her there to discuss which shifts she has to do.

Waitress

Jacki's most important waitressing *duties* are:

- Seating customers
- Taking orders
- Serving food and drinks
- Taking payments
- Clearing and resetting tables
- Preparing the *buffet table*
- Sweeping the restaurant floor

About 30 people work at the restaurant, but most of them are part-timers. There are only four other staff who work full-time like Jacki.

In some ways, Jacki has not one job, but two! Most of the time she works as a waitress, serving in the two-floor restaurant, but sometimes she works in the kitchen instead, making pizzas.

Jacki has been waitressing in the restaurant for almost three years.

When Jacki arrives in the morning for a waitressing **shift**, her main job is to put out the food on the buffets and salad bars. Jacki washes her hands before she fills the two salad bars.

Like all the staff in the restaurant, Jacki scrubs her hands before handling any food.

Jacki wheels some pizza bases into the proving oven.

The chef prepares to bake the first pizzas of the day. All the ingredients arrive at the restaurant in delivery vans, which turn up about twice a week. The pizza dough comes on tall trolleys, frozen in ready-rolled circles. It is taken out of the freezer to defrost overnight, then put into the **proving oven** to rise in the morning.

ost of the pizza toppings and salads are delivered to the restaurant ready-prepared in tubs. But a few ingredients, such as cucumbers and tomatoes, need to be freshly chopped – otherwise they would dry out or go soft.

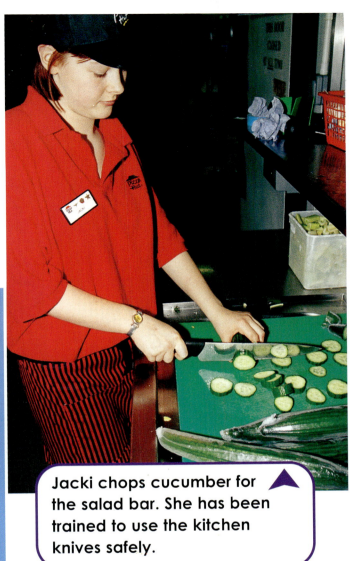

Jacki chops cucumber for the salad bar. She has been trained to use the kitchen knives safely.

JUST THE JOB!

Kitchen Staff

When Jacki works in the kitchen, her duties include:

- Cleaning the kitchens
- Checking deliveries
- Making starters and pizzas to order
- Sending food up in the lift
- Emptying the *potwash* (lift for dirty dishes)
- Loading the dishwasher

The kitchen is in the basement of the building, and the staff send the food up to the restaurant in a lift. Each pizza is sliced into six before it goes into the lift. This makes it easier for customers to help themselves from the buffet.

Quiet Moments

Usually, when Jacki arrives for her waitressing shift the tables are already set. Whoever was working the evening before – possibly Jacki herself – cleared and set them as the customers left. Even so, Jacki still has to check that all the tables have salt and pepper, and that the chilli shakers are full.

Jacki checks that each place setting has a knife, fork and paper napkin.

Favourite Five

Jacki's favourite pizzas are:
1. **Pepperoni Feast (pepperoni with extra cheese)**
2. **Vegetable Supreme (mushroom, peppers and mozzarella)**
3. **Meat Feast (spicy pork, beef, ham and pepperoni)**
4. **Chicken Feast (spicy chicken)**
5. **Farmhouse (ham and mushroom)**

Once the restaurant is ready for the customers, Jacki can have an early lunch break. She tucks in to her free pizza and soft drink when most people would be having their morning coffee break! But when the restaurant opens at 11 a.m. Jacki will be rushed off her feet. She probably won't have another chance to sit down for hours.

Jacki and Steve, the Assistant Manager, enjoy their free pizza while the restaurant is still closed.

Essential Kit

Jacki has to look neat and tidy for the customers. Her uniform consists of:

- Pizza Hut top
- Name badge
- Pizza Hut apron for carrying her order notebook and pencil
- Bumbag for storing any *tips*
- Black trousers (her own)
- Black shoes (her own)

When she works in the kitchen she has to wear a hat, too.

Jacki takes a pile of clean pizza plates to each table.

There to Serve

W hen Jacki is on a waitressing shift, work starts getting busy around 11.30 a.m. When customers come in, the first job is to show them to their table. Jacki picks up menus on the way and hands them to the customers when they are comfortably seated.

The restaurant has special high chairs for its youngest customers!

There are special menus for young children, and usually something to stop them getting bored, such as a place mat to colour in and some crayons. If there is a baby in the party, Jacki fetches a high chair.

acki takes any orders for drinks first, so she can leave the customers to study the menu. When she comes back she writes down their pizza order in her notebook, then keys it into the till.

Glenn and Jason are regulars. They always order the same favourite pizzas, but Jacki still reads back their order just to be sure.

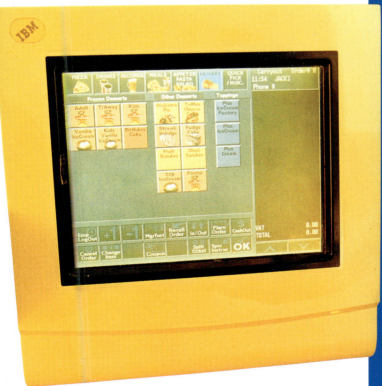

The till is very user-friendly. It has a *touch-screen* and picture keys.

Top Tips

Jacki went on a training course for waitressing, so she knows what she must ask the customers and never misses anything out:

- Write down the drinks order
- Bring back the drinks
- Take the pizza order
- Check if the customers want any side orders, such as salads
- Read back the order to prevent any mistakes
- Key the order into the till

In the Kitchens

When Jacki keys the order in to the till, it automatically prints out on a machine in the kitchen. Ches, the chef, hangs the order up by a peg where everyone can see it. The kitchen staff start preparing the food without delay. Of course, on the days that Jacki is on kitchen duty, it is her job to make the pizzas!

The orders print out in the kitchen. They are pegged up so the staff know which dishes to prepare. ▲

Matt takes some bubbling garlic bread with cheese out of the oven. ▲

The kitchen staff aim to have starters ready within five minutes of the order, so items such as garlic bread are cooked first. Pizzas are ready within 15 minutes, which gives the customers time to eat their first course.

Pizza Chef

Ches can prepare a pizza for the grill in under a minute!

- **Take the circle of proven dough**
- **Spread the surface with tomato mix**
- **Sprinkle on the grated cheese**
- **Add the right toppings**
- **Grill – until the cheese bubbles!**

Top Tips

Food safety is extremely important. The kitchen staff must:

- **Wear a hat**
- **Wash their hands**
- **Not let raw ingredients touch cooked ones**
- **Check the use-by dates on the food in the walk-in fridge**
- **Not let cooked meats stay *unrefrigerated* for too long**

This is Ches, the pizza chef. All the toppings are ready-chopped so that he can prepare the pizzas quickly.

When an order is ready, it is placed in the food lift. The print-out from the till is sent up with it, so that Jacki knows which table to take it to.

Jacki helps out in the kitchen by loading the dishwasher with dirty pizza pans.

Help Yourself

Customers who want to help themselves to salad need bowls. Jacki asks whether they want a regular or large helping of salad, then brings the bowls while the customers are waiting for their pizza.

Jacki checks on the salad bar each time she passes it. If a certain item is running low, she calls down to the kitchen so that staff there can send up a refill tub in the lift. She wipes away any spills whenever she gets a chance. The customers can make quite a mess, especially with the salad dressings!

Best Sellers

Jacki normally knows which salad items will run out first. The most popular are:

1. Potato salad
2. Coleslaw
3. Pasta salad
4. Grated carrot
5. Bacon bits

Jacki is responsible for keeping the salad bar clean and well-stocked.

If customers have **opted for** the pizza buffet, Jacki explains that they can help themselves to as many slices of pizza as they can eat, then goes to fetch them their drinks order. As with the salad bar, Jacki checks that no item runs out.

Jacki has to be careful not to spill the drinks she is carrying. ▶

◀ Jacki brings fresh pizzas to the buffet table through the day. Customers have a wide choice whatever time they turn up.

Pizzas and Puddings

All the waiters and waitresses watch the light on the food lift. When it goes on, that means some food has been sent up from the kitchen. The staff use special, *insulated* metal grippers to pick up the piping-hot pizza pans. They don't have time to keep putting on oven gloves and then taking them off.

Who Ordered What?

Jacki has no trouble remembering which orders go to which customers:

• All the tables are numbered, and the table number is printed on the food order slip.

• Each waiter or waitress looks after particular tables, either in the ground or first floor restaurant.

• Notable features, such as the colour of a customer's top or even the shape of their nose, help Jacki to remember orders, too!

Jacki takes the hot pizza pans out of the food lift. These ones are for customers being served by Sati, one of the waiters.

When Jacki takes pizzas to one of her tables, she checks on the customers' drinks. She brings fresh ones if people are still thirsty. Jacki keeps an eye on all the tables that she is serving. When she is sure that everyone has finished eating, she clears away the dirty dishes and asks if anyone wants to see a dessert menu. She serves desserts, brings coffees, and finally brings the bill.

Making dessert can be an artistic affair! Jacki has a huge choice of toppings for decorating ice cream from the machine.

It's not pleasant clearing up other people's mess.

Not all customers come in for a sit-down meal. When Jacki is working in the ground floor restaurant, she often serves takeaway pizzas too. These are more common in the early evening, when people are on their way home from work.

Jacki gives the customer her takeaway pizzas. The cardboard boxes keep the pizzas warm.

Tricky Moments

Many customers pay for their meal with a bank card or a cheque. With these payments, Jacki has to be certain that the customer's signature matches the one on the card. With cheques, Jacki must write the guarantee card number on the back, and also make sure that the customer has filled it in properly, even down to writing the correct date and year.

Jacki's own working day can last until 10, 10.30 or even 11.30 p.m, depending on the day of the week. There are fewer customers later in the evening, so Jacki gets a chance to load dirty dishes into the potwash, set the tables for the next day and mop the floor. This can be especially messy around the salad bar.

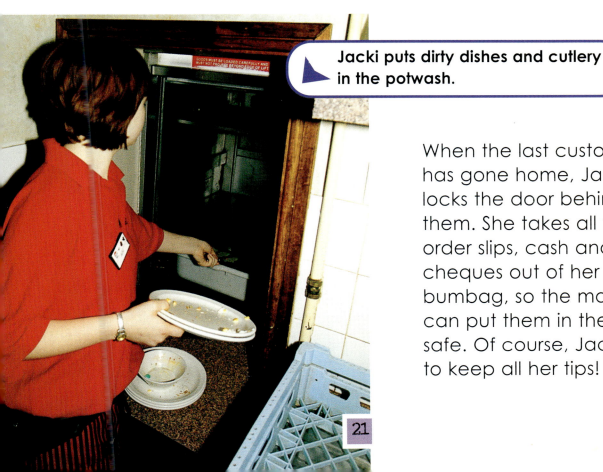

▶ **Jacki puts dirty dishes and cutlery in the potwash.**

When the last customer has gone home, Jacki locks the door behind them. She takes all the order slips, cash and cheques out of her bumbag, so the manager can put them in the till or safe. Of course, Jacki gets to keep all her tips!

Pros ...

For Jacki, the best thing about working in the restaurant is the **flexible** hours. She likes being part of a young, friendly team and the variety of doing some shifts in the kitchen.

Jacki likes being part of a team. Here she is with Adam, Sati and Steve.

Tips from the customers are a perk of the job.

Jacki is paid weekly, and the money goes directly into her bank account, but she also gets extra money on top – the tips that customers give to reward her good service. Of course, she receives paid holiday, and she never has to work on Christmas Day or Boxing Day because the restaurant is closed on those days.

There are other perks, too, such as all the free pizza and soft drinks while she is at work. If Jacki goes into the restaurant in her free time with a group of friends, four of the meals are half price – which makes her very popular!

Working for a **chain** rather than an individual restaurant has its advantages. There is lots of organised training and it is easy to plot your own **career path**. Jacki is about to go on a course to be a Star Trainer. After this, she will be able to train up new recruits. That means a **promotion** and a pay rise. Jacki will then start working towards being a Manager, and then a Restaurant General Manager like Jo.

Open for Business

The working day begins a couple of hours before the restaurant opens and continues until just after it closes. If Jacki's on a late shift, she doesn't have to get in until lunch time!

... and Cons

Jacki's shifts are about nine hours long, and she can get very tired being on her feet all day. Unfortunately, the times when Jacki would really like a break or a bite to eat are the times that the restaurant is busiest.

Jacki's least favourite job is emptying the rubbish into the outdoor *skip*. When it's full, the skip really stinks.

The worst part of the job is clearing up after the customers. There is nothing worse than other people's leftovers, and some people leave a revolting mess. This can put Jacki off her free pizza – though of course, she realises that it is not good to eat pizza all the time anyway!

Top Tips

Jacki has her own routine for clearing a table:

- **Stack all the dirty dishes**
- **Wipe the worst of the mess into one of the dishes**
- **Carry the dishes to the potwash and pile them in**
- **Return to the table to wipe it with *anti-bacterial* spray**
- **Use a fresh cloth to dry the table**

Although Jacki is a naturally cheerful, happy person, even she finds it hard to keep smiling sometimes – especially when customers are rude, or even just slow and **indecisive**. It can be difficult trying to hurry customers along when there is a queue of people waiting for a table. When customers are really badly-behaved, though, Jacki asks Jo or Steve to come and deal with them.

Sometimes the customers can get quite rowdy, but Jacki has been trained to deal with people *assertively*.

Finally, Jacki is not keen on wearing a uniform. It helps that she can wear her own trousers and shoes, but she feels a bit embarrassed wearing the **regulation** top when her friends come in!

Emptying the glass dishwasher in the bar can be hot, sticky work, particularly on a warm summer afternoon.

Finding a Job

The only **qualifications** for working at a restaurant are that, like Jacki, you are hard-working and friendly. It really is essential that you get on with people, because you are dealing with them all the time. This is not so important if you work in the kitchens, but even there you will need to get on with the other staff.

Jacki gets on well with her mum, Jill, who also works at the restaurant.

A good memory is a big help, and not just for the food orders. You need to remember the training you are given and put it into practice. If you are a clumsy person, then maybe a career in a restaurant isn't for you.

Jacki has a locker where she can store her uniform if she doesn't need to take it home for washing.

It's Danny's first day at work. He empties the dishwasher in the bar area and puts away the clean glasses.

Job Know-How

What qualifications do I need?

None in most fast-food restaurants, although you have to attend training sessions as part of the job. In other restaurants, kitchen staff are expected to have some cookery qualifications.

What personal qualities do I need?

Polite and friendly. Lots of *stamina* and a strong stomach (for clearing up people's mess, not for eating pizza!). A good memory.

How do I apply?

Ask at the restaurant branch nearest to your home, or look out for adverts in the local papers.

Will there be an interview?

Yes. This is to make sure that you will be able to deal with the customers. But if you are not very confident with people, you might be able to start out by working in the kitchens.

The best way to gain experience of working in a restaurant is to take on a part-time job. Next time you go for a meal, ask the manager how to apply. If you do this, there will probably be a full-time position for you when you leave school – like there was for Jacki.

27

Glossary

Anti-bacterial	Something that destroys bacteria (germs).
Assertively	With firmness and confidence.
Buffet table	Heated counter where people can help themselves to food.
Career path	The series of jobs that make up a person's career.
Chain	Describes a group of restaurants that have branches in several different towns. All the restaurants in a chain have the same name, the same items on the menu and the same opportunities for their staff.
Duties	Jobs that must be done.
Flexible	Not fixed.
Guarantee card	Card issued by a bank that guarantees (promises) a cheque will be paid.
Indecisive	Unable to make up one's mind.
Insulated	Describes a material that does not allow heat to pass through it.
Opted for	Chosen the option of.
Perk	An extra advantage that comes with a job.
Potwash	The lift that carries dirty dishes to the kitchen.
Promotion	Moving up to a job with more responsibility and/or better pay
Proving oven	A warm (not hot) oven that is used to make dough rise.
Qualifications	Official requirements for a particular job.
Regulation	Describes an item, such as part of a uniform, that obeys all the rules.
Shift	The period of time someone works in a day.
Skip	A metal container used as a giant bin for rubbish.
Stamina	Strength; the ability to carry on despite being tired.
Tips	Money given to thank a waiter or waitress for their good service.
Touch-screen	A computer screen that shows different 'buttons' that respond to touch.
Unrefrigerated	Not chilled in a fridge.
Work experience	An unpaid period of work, often for a week, so that a person can see what a job is like at first-hand

Find Out More

Have a meal at the restaurant where Jacki works:

Pizza Hut
Briggate
Leeds
WEST YORKSHIRE LS1 6HD

Visit these websites to find out more about chain restaurants in the United Kingdom. Many have a page of 'recruitment' where you can find out about job opportunities:

www.burgerking.co.uk
www.deeppanpizza.co.uk
www.garfunkels.co.uk
www.mcdonalds.co.uk
www.pizzaexpress.co.uk
www.pizzahut.co.uk
www.tgifridays.co.uk

Become a pizza expert! Try an internet search on the word 'pizza' or visit the 'Pizza-pedia' webpage, which has links to a history of pizza, recipes and much, much more:

www.geocities.com/Heartland/ Flats/5353/pizza/

Find out more about further qualifications by visiting the NVQ website:

www.dfee.gov.uk/nvq

In Australia and New Zealand you can check out:

www.pizzahut.com.au
www.mcdonalds.com.au
www.hungryjacks.com.au
Restaurant Association of New Zealand – **www.restaurantnz.co.nz**
Pizza Hut – (NZ) 09-3094442
McDonalds (NZ) 09-3065600

Also, why don't you…

- Visit your local library and check out the careers section.

- Find out if there is a teacher at your school who is an expert careers advisor.

- Check with the manager at your local restaurant to see if there are any vacancies.

- Look in your local business directory under 'Restaurants' to find out whom to contact for *work experience* placements.

Index